Git Academy

Master Advanced Version Control Techniques

Table of Contents

Chapter 1. Introduction

In the realm of version control, Git reigns supreme for its robustness, versatility, and ubiquity with businesses and developers globally. As such, our special report, "Git Academy: Master Advanced Version Control Techniques", provides the comprehensive, insightful guide to elevate your skills beyond simple commits and merges. This report is not just another technical handbook, but a key that unlocks profound understanding and efficient application of Git's finest tools. Crafted in a digestible yet exhaustive manner, it is aimed not only at veterans seeking to deepen their prowess but also at neophytes longing to enhance their proficiency. Step into a mastery of Version Control, optimize your workflow, and become a sought-after professional in your field. After all, in today's tech-driven world, becoming adept in cutting-edge tools like Git is more than just a skill - it's a career booster. Discover the nuances of advanced version control techniques with Git Academy and build your software development future today.

Chapter 2. Demystifying Git's Underlying Mechanics

In understanding the superior tool that is Git, it is important to delve beneath the surface and explore the mechanism that powers its efficient version control attributes.

2.1. Git Objects

One of Git's foundational principles is data as files and directories snapshot. Git objects are the core around which Git revolves. You find four basic types here: blobs, trees, commits, and tags.

A **blob** is used to store file data. It is fundamentally a file with a filename. Blobs are immutable and once a blob is created, it cannot be changed.

Trees in Git are akin to directories. They serve as containers for blobs and other trees, essentially mirroring the file system of directories, subdirectories, and files.

A **commit** object holds metadata for each change introduced into the repository including the author, committer, date, and a pointer to the tree object representing the top directory for the committed project's snapshot.

Tags reference a specific commit. A tag object is very much like a commit object – it contains a tagger (the person who created the tag), the date and time, a message, and a pointer.

2.2. Git Branching Model

Branching and merging are at the heart of Git's essence. Each commit in Git carries a link to its parent commit(s). A branch in git is nothing more than a lightweight movable pointer to one of these commits.

Creating a new branch creates a new pointer for you to move around. The default branch name in Git is `master`. As you start making commits, you're given a master branch that points to the latest commit you've made. Whenever you commit, the master branch pointer moves forward automatically.

Git does not create an entirely new copy of the existing code base when you create a branch, instead, Git uses the commit history stored as snapshots to recreate the directory structure of the project.

2.3. Git's SHA-1 Hashes

A SHA-1 hash is a unique identifier generated by an algorithm. In the world of Git, each commit is uniquely identified by a SHA-1 hash. This hash is used as the pointer to parent commit(s), a blob, or a tree.

When you make changes, Git generates a new SHA-1 hash because, remember, Git stores content, not differences. Each file version and commits get their unique SHA-1 hash.

2.4. Git's Distributed Nature

Git's design as a distributed version control system is fundamental to its efficiency and control. Unlike centralized version control systems that depend on network access to a central server, each Git repository on every computer is a full-fledged repository with complete history and version-tracking abilities, independent of network access or a central server.

Changes are stored as patches that can be synchronized between different repositories. This approach enables working offline, parallel work flows, and scales to large projects.

Each developer gets a local copy and full control of the entire project's history, and operations are performed locally. This introduces significant speed and efficiency.

2.5. Git's Three-stage Workflow

Git's workflow involves three stages: the working directory, the staging area, and the repository (.git directory).

The working directory is a single checkout of one version of the project. These files are pulled out of the compressed database in the Git directory and placed on disk for you to use or modify.

The staging area, also known as the "index", is an area where we can place our files to prepare them to be committed to the Git repository.

The `.git` directory is where Git stores everything it needs to keep track of the repository's history. Once you've staged changes, you commit them to your Git directory.

To conclude, understanding the underlying mechanics of Git is vital to getting the most out of the system. From objects and hashes to branches and workflow stages, these components collectively underpin one of the most powerful version control systems available. As you continue your journey through Git Academy, look forward to honing your grasp of these mechanics and transforming your overall Git skillset.

Chapter 3. Advancing Beyond Basic Commands: Git from Intermediate to Expert

Get ready to expand your Git capabilities beyond the essentials to understand the advanced uses of various commands and workflows with this comprehensive guide. Going through this material, you'll find yourself transitioning from an experienced user to an expert in using Git for your every coding and collaboration need.

3.1. Reflog and Detached HEAD State

The `git reflog` command is your last resort for recovering lost commits, and it serves as a log history for every action. It's a list of all actions in a repository and provides a fantastic safety net.

Here's how you can apply reflog:

```
git reflog
```

A detached HEAD state essentially means that 'HEAD' is not pointing to the last commit of the current branch.

A detached HEAD state is entered under these circumstances: `git checkout commit`, `git checkout new_branch` where `new_branch` does not yet exist, `git rebase`.

To recover from a detached HEAD:

```
git checkout master # or another existing branch
```

3.2. Cherry Picking

Cherry picking in Git means to choose a commit from one branch and apply it onto another. This makes it possible to take useful commits to new branches that need changes.

To cherry-pick a commit:

```
git cherry-pick <commit-hash>
```

3.3. Rebasing and The Three-Way Merge

Rebase allows you to move or combine a sequence of commits to a new base commit. It's great for avoiding unnecessary merges while cleaning up commits and making them more understandable for others.

To perform a rebase:

```
git rebase <branch>
```

By using `git rebase`, you can also squash multiple commits into one. This is handy in making your Git history cleaner.

A three-way merge is a merge that uses 3 commits; base, ours, and theirs. Git merges these three points in two steps: the base to ours (current branch pointer), and the base to theirs (the branch to be merged).

Implementing a three-way merge:

```
git merge <branch>
```

3.4. GIT Workflows

There are numerous ways workflows can be designed: Centralized, Feature Branch, Gitflow, Forking.

- Centralized: Changes are shared via a central repository. Developers clone the central repo and work directly off master.

- Feature Branch: Each new feature resides in its own branch, which can be pushed to central repo for backup/collaboration. There's a risk that the master branch may have advanced, generating conflicts with your changes.

- Gitflow: It assigns specific roles to different branches and defines how and when they should interact. Feature branches are integrated into the main code.

- Forking: It's the standard way of using community-orientated public projects on GitHub.

3.5. Advanced Tips for Troubleshooting

Learn how to exit Vim (`:q!`), fix mistakes with `commit --amend`, discard changes in your working directory (`checkout -- .` or `stash`), unmodifying a modified file (`checkout -- file`), unstaging a file (`reset HEAD <file>`), host your code with versions on GitHub, Bitbucket, or Gitlab.

3.6. Git Bisect

Bisect helps find the commit that introduced a bug by using binary search.

Usage:

```
# start the process
git bisect start

# define the bad commit
git bisect bad <bad_commit>

# define old known good commit
git bisect good <old_known_good_commit>

# bisect runs binary search
git bisect run <my_script>

# bisect resets the HEAD to the current branch
git bisect reset
```

In conclusion, mastering Git is key to efficient version control and collaborative development. With these advanced techniques, you're now ready to optimize your workflow and become a sought-after Git expert in your field.

Keep in mind this journey has more to offer. Share your experiences and continue your exploration - Git is a tool that never ceases to evolve and improve.

Chapter 4. Mastering the Art of Branching and Merging

Branching and merging represent two fundamental aspects of Git version control. Known for their power and flexibility, these techniques enable the uncomplicated testing of new features and ensure quick and painless integration of changes.

4.1. Understanding the Concept of Branching

Branching represents the creation of an identical copy of your code, on which you can experiment and make changes without affecting the main, or 'master', branch. This characteristic is particularly useful when developing a new feature or attempting to fix a bug.

To create a branch, use the command below:

```
$ git branch Branch_Name
```

This command only creates a new branch but doesn't switch you to it. To switch to the new branch you just created or any other existing branch, use the command:

```
$ git checkout Branch_Name
```

Although it is common to use the above two commands separately, there is a shortcut command which accomplishes both tasks in a single line:

```
$ git checkout -b Branch_Name
```

Here, the -b option stands for branch, indicating the creation of a new branch and switching to it immediately.

4.2. Navigating and Inspecting Branches

Knowing how to create and switch between branches is crucial, but you will also need to view existing branches and observe differences between them.

To list all existing branches, use the command:

```
$ git branch
```

This command lists all available branches and marks the current working branch with an asterisk (*).

To compare differences between two branches, use the git diff command:

```
$ git diff Branch1_Name..Branch2_Name
```

Understanding how your branches differ is vital to manage changes effectively and avoid conflicts.

4.3. Making Changes and Committing

Now that we understand how to create, checkout, and compare branches, we can discuss changes. In a branch, any change made to the project will only affect that branch, leaving the master untouched.

To commit changes, you can use Git's standard add and commit commands:

```
$ git add File_Name
$ git commit -m "Commit Message"
```

Upon running these commands, changes will only apply to your current branch.

4.4. Understanding Merging

Merging is the process of integrating changes from one branch into another—typically the master branch. This method of integrating changes is a powerful tool for collaborative work environments, where various features or fixes are developed on separate branches.

To merge changes from a specified branch to the current branch, switch to the target branch where you want to integrate the changes, and run:

```
$ git merge Branch_Name
```

This command initiates a three-way merge, creating a new commit in the current branch that includes all changes from the specified branch.

4.5. Handling Merge Conflicts

Occasionally, when two people change the same part of the same file at the same time, merge conflicts may occur. Git can't decide which change is the correct one, and it requires human intervention to resolve the conflict.

When a conflict arises, Git will present a message upon attempting to merge:

```
$ git merge Branch_Name
Auto-merging File_Name
CONFLICT (content): Merge conflict in File_Name
Automatic merge failed; fix conflicts and then commit
the result.
```

The conflicting file will contain conflict markers that indicate the differing sections. It's your responsibility to resolve these conflicts either manually or with a merge tool, and then commit the changes.

In mastering the art of branching and merging in Git, you will gain a high degree of control over modifications to your projects, significantly increasing your ability to manage and collaborate on complex projects. This knowledge also places you at the heart of one of the most utilized and powerful systems in the current coding industry—making you an indispensable asset in any development team.

Remember—like any craft, mastery comes with practice. Don't be afraid to experiment with branches and merges, create fictional conflicts to better understand how to resolve them, and commit changes frequently to cement your understanding.

Chapter 5. Navigating Troublesome Waters: Error Handling and Recovery in Git

From time to time, every developer runs into problems when using Git. Lost commits, detached HEADs, overwritten files, and more can cause much frustration. To help you traverse these troublesome waters, we'll guide you through some common problems and their solutions. They key to solving these issues often lies in understanding how Git operates under the hood, be efficient with your workflow, and utilizing some lesser known commands.

5.1. Understanding Git's Internals for Effective Error Handling

Before diving into specific error-handling practices, it's crucial to understand certain Git internals—knowledge of which will lead you to make more sense of error messages and find effective solutions.

5.1.1. Git Objects

Git's object model consists of blobs (file data), trees (directories of blobs and trees), and commits (refs to trees with metadata); each object has a SHA-1 hash as its unique identifier.

5.1.2. The Staging Area

Git utilizes a two-step commit process. Any changes moved into the 'staging area' (technically called "the index") are to be included in the next commit.

5.1.3. Git Branches

In reality, a Git branch is simply a pointer to a commit. The default branch in Git repository is typically known as `master`.

5.1.4. The HEAD Pointer

The HEAD pointer is especially important to understand—it points to the tip of the current branch in your local repository.

With these fundamentals in mind, you can better understand error messages and potential problem situations arise when working Git. Now, let's move on to common errors and the ways to solve them.

5.2. Rescuing Lost Commits

If you ever find a commit that's no longer part of any branch, don't panic. Git provides a safety net in the form of the reflog, a log of where your HEAD and branch references have pointed in the past.

To access the reflog, use the command `git reflog`. The reflog is organized in reverse chronological order, so the most recent operation is at the top. Once you've found the commit you denoted as lost, you can create a new branch pointing at it to rescue it:

```
$ git branch rescue-branch <SHA-1 of the lost commit>
```

5.3. Recovering from a Detached HEAD

If you check out a commit that is not the latest commit of any branch, Git will issue a warning that you are in a "detached HEAD" state.

Essentially, this means you're no longer on a particular branch but on an anonymous branch created when you checked out a particular commit. Any new commits created in this state aren't reflected in any other branch, and can be lost once you check out a named branch. Here's what you can do:

1. If you haven't made any commits in the detached HEAD state and want to return to the latest commit of your last checked-out branch, run `git checkout -`.

2. If you created new commits and want them on a new branch, run `git checkout -b <new-branch-name>`.

5.4. Dealing with Merge Conflicts

Merging branches is a common operation in Git, but it can also lead to conflicts—especially when the same part of a file has been changed differently in two branches.

When you encounter a merge conflict, Git will pause the merge operation and alert you that there are conflicts to resolve.

Then, you can use various tools (like `git diff`) to identify and resolve these conflicts by deciding which changes to keep and which to discard.

Once you've resolved the conflicts, use `git add .` to mark the files as resolved. Then you can continue the merge with `git commit`.

5.5. Restoring Overwritten Files

If you've accidentally overwritten a file and haven't yet committed the changes, Git can help you restore the file to its most recent committed state.

To restore a file to how it looks in the last commit, run:

```
$ git checkout -- <file>
```

It's important not to confuse this with the `git checkout <branch>` command, which switches branches.

In conclusion, understanding how Git's internals work and knowing about commands that are not commonly used allows you to handle Git errors more efficiently. Always keep in mind that Git rarely loses data, and there's usually a way to recover, often through `reflog` or carefully examining the commit history. This resilience is one of the reasons why Git is the preferred version control system for so many developers. Don't be afraid of errors; instead, learn to navigate these troublesome waters, and you will eventually master Git.

Remember that a mistake or error can turn into an opportunity to learn something new about Git, which will surely contribute to your proficiency and help you become a sought-after professional in the field of software development. Happy coding!

Chapter 6. Juggling Multiple Projects: An Insight to Submodules and Subtrees

Version control is crucial when working on multiple projects and can be immensely simplified utilizing Git's advanced features, particularly submodules and subtrees. By gaining proficiency in these tools, you ensure efficient juggling of several projects, simultaneously maintaining their individuality and providing seamless integration.

6.1. Understanding Submodules

Submodules allow you to include or embed one or more Git repositories within a parent repository, keeping your projects separable yet interconnected. This is particularly useful when dependent on external libraries or other projects. Let's dig into how to create, update, and manage submodules.

6.1.1. Initializing a Submodule

To initialize a submodule, navigate to your project's root directory and utilize the following syntax:

```
git submodule add [URL] [path-to-place-the-submodule]
```

Replace '[URL]' with the Git URL of the project you'll be incorporating as a submodule. '[path-to-place-the-submodule]' must be replaced with the location within your project where the submodule should exist.

6.1.2. Updating Submodules

After initialization, remember that submodules will not update automatically with a 'git pull' or 'git fetch' in the parent repository. Update a submodule by traversing into the submodule directory and running:

```
git pull origin [branch-name]
```

6.1.3. Managing Submodules

If your parent repository contains several submodules and updating each individually seems inefficient, consider the 'foreach' keyword. This Git command iterates through all initialized submodules and applies the 'git pull' command:

```
git submodule foreach git pull origin [branch-name]
```

6.2. Embracing Subtrees

While submodules incorporate a separate project preserving its history, a subtree allows you to fold a project into your repository as a sub-directory, combining the project histories. Following are the steps to work with subtrees.

6.2.1. Adding a Subtree

Use the 'git subtree add' command to include a project as a sub-directory:

```
git subtree add --prefix=[sub-directory-name]
```

```
[repository-url] [branch-name]
```

Remember to use the appropriate repository URL, the destination sub-directory, and the correct branch name of the repository to be added.

6.2.2. Updating a Subtree

Perhaps you wish to pull the changes from the added project repository to your subtree. In this case, use the 'git subtree pull' command:

```
git subtree pull --prefix=[sub-directory-name]
[repository-url] [branch-name]
```

Make sure to replace '[sub-directory-name]', '[repository-url]', and '[branch-name]' with the correct values.

6.2.3. Pushing Changes to Subtree

Sometimes, you'll want to push changes you made in the subtree to the original repository. To do this, use 'git subtree push:

```
git subtree push --prefix=[sub-directory-name]
[repository-url] [branch-name]
```

6.3. Submodules vs. Subtrees: Making the Choice

Deciding between submodules and subtrees depends on your project intricacy and needs. Submodules are superb when you need to preserve complete standalone projects under your main project without merging histories, especially when these projects are being independently developed. On the other hand, subtrees excellently perform when you want to include another project into yours while maintaining the ability to push changes back upstream and having a simpler interaction model.

6.4. Conclusion

Handling multiple projects does not have to be a daunting task. With Git's submodules and subtrees, you can manage numerous projects, making your development workflow more flexible and streamlined. Understanding when to use either is vital, and through practice, your proficiency will grow, supplementing your professional toolkit.

Chapter 7. Power Play: Leveraging the Strength of Rebasing

Even amidst the myriad of Git commands, `rebase` stands tall as a potent tool that allows developers to streamline their project history. This command allows us to rearrange and manage commit history in a more linear and tidy manner, making it easier to comprehend what's happening over time. However, its capability extends well beyond a mere cleaner history. It can also be finely tuned to bring forth alterations in existing commits, squash, split, and even reorder them. Let's dive into the depths and discover the might of rebasing with Git.

7.1. Understanding Git Rebase

To begin with, let's briefly explain what rebasing is. It involves moving or combining a sequence of commits to a new base commit. Compared with traditional merging, which adds a new commit in your project history while preserving the context and date of the original commits, rebasing rewrites the project history by creating new commits for each commit in the original branch. While this can make your project history more streamlined, it also means the context of these commits will be changed.

7.2. Basic Git Rebase

When you first start using rebase, it's essential to become familiar with the base command, `git rebase <branch>`. This moves the entire current branch on top of the specified base branch. One common use case for this is keeping feature branches up-to-date with the latest changes from the main branch.

Here's how you can use it:

```
git checkout feature_branch
git rebase main
```

7.3. Interactive Rebasing

Interactive rebase or `git rebase -i` is where the power of rebasing truly shines. The `-i` flag opens a UI that allows you to modify commits as they move to the new base.

The most common form is as follows:

```
git rebase -i HEAD~n
```

where `n` is the number of commits from `HEAD` backwards you want to modify.

This command opens your default text editor with the last `n` commits:

```
pick 1fc6c95 do something
pick 6b2481b do something else
pick dd1475d changed some things
...
```

Every commit is prefixed with the word `pick`, implying they'll be moved without changes. However, you can replace `pick` with a command, such as `reword`, `edit`, `squash`, `fixup` or `drop`, followed by the desired modifications.

7.4. Power Commands in Interactive Rebasing

Every command in the rebasing UI serves a unique purpose and allows you to sculpt your commits to your liking.

`reword`: This command lets you alter commit messages. In the text editor, replace `pick` with `reword` for the chosen commit.

`edit`: This powerful command suspends rebase at that commit, allowing you to modify that commit any way you want: add new content, modify or remove something, or even split it into multiple commits.

`squash` and `fixup`: Both commands are used to merge commits together. `squash` combines this commit with the previous one and offers you to write a new commit message. `fixup` also combines the commit with the previous one but discards the current commit message.

`drop`: Simply removes the commit completely.

7.5. Handling Rebase Conflicts

During rebasing, you might encounter conflicts if changes from the two branches overlap. Refrain from panic at this stage; resolve the conflicts as you typically would, stage the changes with `git add`, and then use `git rebase --continue`.

In case you want to abort the whole process, use `git rebase --abort`, and Git will return your branch to its state prior to initiating the rebase.

7.6. Rebasing Vs Merging

Despite its potency, `rebase` is not always the correct tool to use. Discern whether to use `merge` or `rebase` wisely, taking into consideration the project requirements, team agreement, and the consequences each method brings about on the project history landscape.

Remember that while `rebase` provides a clean, linear history, it rewrites history. This can be an issue when working on public branches. On the other hand, `merge` maintains the context of an overall feature development and makes it explicit when and how a certain decision was incorporated in the project.

To conclude, `rebase` is a versatile tool that, when used judiciously, can make your version control much more effective and succinct. However, it does come with its caveats, and therefore must always be used cautiously and conscientiously. Through time and practice, you are sure to leverage the full power of rebasing and emerge a master in version control.

Chapter 8. Implementing Efficient Workflow Strategies with Git

Version control has evolved to be a critical component of software development, and mastering Git can immensely optimize your workflow. Efficient workflow strategies with Git revolve around three crucial areas: branch management, commit structure, and merge strategies. Mastering these is the key to unlocking your Git prowess.

8.1. Understanding Branch Management

Branch management is an integral part of managing changes and improvements to the software without disturbing its operational state. No matter if you're working alone on a project or with a team, branch management helps keep your code organized and your development flow optimal.

Creating a new branch for every new feature or bug fix is good practice. The `git branch` command is used to manage branches in Git.

```
$ git branch new-feature-branch
```

You can then switch to your new branch using the `git checkout` command.

```
$ git checkout new-feature-branch
```

For a more straightforward workflow, you can create a new branch and switch to it using the -b option in a single command.

```
$ git checkout -b new-feature-branch
```

Remember to keep your branches small and focused on a single feature or bug fix for an efficient Git workflow.

8.2. Producing Effective Commit Structure

Commit structure is paramount to efficient workflow strategies. Each commit should represent a coherent set of changes, whether they belong to more significant changes or a stand-alone improvement. The git commit command is what makes it possible.

Before you commit, it is advisable to view the changes you have made. The git diff command helps with that.

```
$ git diff
```

You can then add changes to your commit using the git add command. If you want to include all changes, you can do so as follows:

```
$ git add .
```

Each commit should be accompanied by a meaningful message. This allows for improved tracking and understanding of the changes introduced.

```
$ git commit -m "Add new feature"
```

8.3. Exploring Merge Strategies

Merge is a method of integrating changes from different branches. While merging, conflicts might occur. Learning to resolve these conflicts is a key skill for efficient workflows.

To merge changes from another branch into the current one, use the `git merge` command.

```
$ git merge source-branch
```

If Git can auto-merge the changes, then no further action is needed; however, if a merge conflict occurs, you will have to manually resolve it.

In cases where conflicts occur, it's important to understand the process of resolution. Git will add conflict markers to the files that have conflicts. These markers look something like this:

```
<<<<<<< HEAD:file.txt
This is the version of the file in your current branch.
=======
This is the version of the file in the branch you are
merging.
>>>>>>> branch-name:file.txt
```

You then need to edit the file to resolve the conflicts, save it, add it to the staging area, and then commit.

8.4. The Role of Pull Requests

Pull requests are a vital part of collaborative software development. They allow developers to collaborate on feature development and integrate changes efficiently.

Pull requests are commonly used in combination with branch policies. This is to ensure that a quality check is performed before changes are merged into a main or release branch.

Using Git and GitHub, the process to create a pull request is simple. First, the changes are pushed to the remote repository.

```
$ git push origin new-feature-branch
```

You can then navigate to the GitHub web interface and open the pull request. This procedure invites others to review your changes.

8.5. Building Efficient Workflows with Git Hooks

Git hooks are scripts that Git executes before or after events such as `commit`, `push`, and `receive`. They're a built-in feature - no need to download anything. Git hooks are a powerful feature for automating aspects of your workflow.

Some common uses include enforcing project build policies, adjusting issues direct from commit messages and checking for consistent style. Make sure that the scripts have the correct permissions to execute, and they are stored in the `.git/hooks` folder.

Learning to leverage Git hooks will undoubtedly streamline various parts of your workflow.

Implementing an efficient Git workflow requires a deep understanding of Git commands and strategies, as well as trial and error in practice. By iterating on your workflow and adopting best practices, you can tailor a workflow that best fits your team's needs and improves overall productivity.

Chapter 9. Cracking the Code: Understanding Git Internals

Version control, particularly with the use of Git, has become an integral part of the modern software development cycle. Designed for efficiency and data integrity, Git is not just about commits, branches, and merges. Its power lies in its intricate internal structure, an understanding of which can enhance your Git proficiency significantly.

9.1. The Underlying Model

The first order of affairs in comprehending Git internals is to understand the model on which Git is based. While many other VCSs store information as a list of file-based changes, Git considers data more like a series of snapshots of a mini file system. Each time you commit, or save the state of your project in Git, it essentially takes a picture of what all your files look like at that moment and stores a reference to that snapshot.

This is an important concept because it means Git maintains a comprehensive history of your projects, a feature that profoundly influences how Git behaves and how data is curated with every action.

9.2. Git as a content-addressable filesystem

Among the pivotal aspects of Git internals is its functionality as a content-addressable filesystem. While it may sound complex, the underlying idea is that Git stores and references data based on the content's hash - a way of creating a unique identifier for digital data, in particular using SHA-1 hash.

It consists of two primary elements: the object, which is stored content, and the reference, which reaches towards this object. Objects can be a blob (the fundamental data type), a tree (which references a blob or another tree), a commit (which indicates trees), and a tag (for marking specific commits).

In simpler terms, when you commit a change, Git creates a new blob object that includes your modifications. It is this storage concept that allows Git to swiftly recall earlier versions of your code.

9.3. Branching in Git

Determined by references, branching in Git is straightforward yet powerful. A branch in Git is merely a lightweight movable pointer to one of these commits. The default branch name in Git is 'master'. As you start making commits, you're given a master branch that points to the last commit you made.

Every time you commit, this pointer moves forward automatically. Adding new branches or switching between them is as instant as updating a pointer, which explains why branching and merging are such painless operations in Git.

9.4. Merging and Deltas

Merging, on the other hand, is the process of integrating changes from various collaborators. Git employs two primary methodologies for merging: Fast Forward and Three-way merging. Fast-forward involves moving the branch pointer ahead, while three-way merges create a new commit that has pointers to the two parent commits it was created from.

Unlike other VCSs, Git doesn't store the differences between commits, also known as deltas. But, when running commands like git gc or git push, Git compresses the data into packfiles. This feature allows Git to work efficiently in storing and retrieving data, even for very large codebases.

9.5. Working with Remotes

Central to Git's collaborative capabilities are remotes - versions of your project that are hosted on the Internet or network somewhere. Collaborating with others involves managing these remote repositories and integrating (pushing and pulling) your work between them. Git allows simultaneous workflow enhancements by letting multiple users work on their copies of the project and syncing changes in diverse directions.

9.6. Hooks and Custom Scripts

Git provides a feature known as 'hooks'. These are custom scripts that git will execute when certain important actions occur. For example, a script can be invoked each time a commit is made, a tag created, or changes pushed or pulled. This opens up an endless realm of possibilities for script automation based on project workflow – from deploying projects to enhanced validation functionality and enforcing project policies.

In conclusion, understanding Git's intricate architecture gives you greater control and insights over your projects— that's what it means to truly embrace the Git mindset. Remember, proficiency in Git is beyond being adept at a range of commands. It's about knowing what happens under the hood, how different components interact, and how they manifest in the versioning of your projects. Knowing Git on a fundamental level broadens your problem-solving spectrum, enhancing not just your skills but your potential as a developer. After all, the skill to control your tools to the fullest is what separates the proficient from the novice.

In the upcoming sections, we will take deeper dives into each of these topics with the intent of sharpening your skills and preparing you to tackle any project with efficiency, no matter its size or complexity.

Chapter 10. Maintaining Security and Integrity with Git

In the realm of version control, certain fundamentals bear extreme importance and out of those, two factors undoubtedly stand top: security and integrity. Understanding how to maintain these in a GIT environment can go a long way in ensuring your software development efforts are safe, efficient, and successful. Let's dive deep.

10.1. Basic Security Principles

Before we delve into the practical application of these principles using Git, a high-level understanding of basic security principles is a must. These principles determine everything from instituting authorized access to maintaining code integrity.

1. Authentication: This is verifying the identity of the user, device, or system who is interacting with your system.

2. Authorization: This checks if an authenticated entity has the correct permissions to perform their intended tasks.

3. Accountability: This tracks actions to the respective identities, ensuring one can be held accountable for their activity.

4. Confidentiality: This ensures that information is accessible only by authorized parties.

5. Integrity: This is reassurance that information will not be altered in transit and arrives exactly as it was sent.

6. Availability: This ascertains that the system is functional and capable of serving authorized entities on-demand.

7. Non-repudiation: This ensures that an entity can't deny the authenticity of their actions.

10.2. Git: A Secure Tool

Git, as a distributed version control system (DVCS), has inherent security mechanisms built into its structure. Most significantly, Git employs the SHA-1 hashing algorithm to secure file and changeset information. Each file and revision is addressed via this hash, proving highly resistant to file corruption, tampering, and password hacks.

Further, Git's model where most operations happen locally rather than over a network is additional security against attacks.

While Git's architecture itself provides a good degree of security, certain practices and tools can bolster your project's protection against unnecessary vulnerabilities.

10.3. Git Configurations for Enhanced Security

Your journey to a more secure Git environment begins with attentiveness to configurations. Simple settings can have a monumental impact.

To verify your identity in Git, use the following commands:

```
$ git config --global user.name "Your Name"
$ git config --global user.email "your.email@domain.com"
```

Avoid storing credentials in plaintext by using Git's built-in credential helper:

```
$ git config --global credential.helper 'store --file
~/.my-credentials'
```

This stores your credentials in a hidden file.

10.4. SSH Keys: Your Lock and Key

Secure Shell (SSH) keys are a secure method of authentication, letting Git establish a secure "tunnel" between your local machine and Git server. SSH keys come in pairs - a private key that remains safely on your machine, and a public key that you upload to the Git server. To generate a new SSH key pair, use the following command:

```
$ ssh-keygen -t rsa -b 4096 -C "your.email@domain.com"
```

Follow the prompt to complete the key generation process. Next, add your key to the SSH-agent:

```
$ eval "$(ssh-agent -s)"
$ ssh-add ~/.ssh/id_rsa
```

To copy your public key to the clipboard, use:

```
$ clip < ~/.ssh/id_rsa.pub
```

Finally, paste it into the SSH keys section in your Git server.

10.5. Managing Permissions with Git

In multi-developer environments, it's crucial that you manage permissions carefully. Roles and responsibilities should be clearly defined and enforced. Git makes this easy through its branching model, where read and write access can be assigned per branch.

The powerful `gitignore` file also enables you to exclude certain files from getting tracked by Git, such as keys, secrets, and environment configuration files. Typically, these are stored in a `.gitignore` file in your project root.

```
# .gitignore
secrets.yml
```

10.6. Code Reviews: An Essential Practice

Code review is a keystone practice in maintaining code integrity and catching potential security flaws. Tools like Pull Requests in GitHub, Merge Requests in GitLab, and Patch-Set in Gerrit offer built-in code review processes that allow developers to scrutinize proposed changes before they're integrated into the mainline.

10.7. Security with Git Hooks

'Git Hooks' are scripts that Git executes before or after events such as commit, push, and receive, further bolstering your defenses. For instance, a pre-commit hook can be used for static code analysis, while a post-receive hook can be utilized for notifying a Continuous Integration server about the recent update.

10.8. Git Submodules and Trees: Points of Vulnerabilities

Git Submodules and Git Trees, while handy in managing third-party code and large files, can pose notable security risks if misused. Always inspect third-party submodules before integrating into your project, and handle merges with care to avoid infiltration by unauthorized code.

The most crucial part of maintaining security and integrity with Git is staying vigilant and proactive. Regularly audit your settings, educate your team on best practices, and stay up-to-date with emerging security concerns in the Git ecosystem.

Maintaining security and integrity in Git and other version control systems involves a blend of understanding, vigilance, and the appropriate use of advanced features. By adopting the measures discussed in this chapter, you can ensure that your codebase remains safe, clean, and optimized for efficient development. In the following chapters, we'll delve into more advanced topics and provide practical walkthroughs to help you master Git's finest tools.

Chapter 11. Future of Version Control: Next Steps after Mastering Git

In this rapidly evolving technological world, the tools and techniques of yesterday might not be all sufficient tomorrow. With Git, you have mastered an invaluable tool built with a strong foundation, but the journey doesn't stop there. The landscape of version control continues to grow and adapt, making it more essential than ever to stay up-to-date and foundationally flexible.

11.1. Adapting to Changes

Version control is never static; it evolves as new challenges and complexities arise in the field of software development. One of the main factors driving the future of version control is the burgeoning growth of data. As projects grow, the sheer amount of data being handled by version control systems raises questions about performance, storage, and integrity of this data.

New responses to these emerging challenges are continually being sought, with concepts such as smart mirroring and sharding being incorporated into version control processes. The future will demand a deeper understanding and adaptation of these more advanced techniques, honing skills beyond regular commits and merges. DevOps culture, Continuous Integration/Continuous Delivery (CI/CD) and automated testing tightly integrate with the version control ecosystem, making it vital to understand and embrace these concepts.

11.2. Advanced Concepts in Version Control

Just as Git brought about a revolution in version control, the advances in distributed version control systems (DVCS) set to project version control into the future. You might wonder, isn't Git a DVCS? Yes, it is, but the landscape might be shifting towards another evolution - the decentralized version of DVCS.

While this concept is in its infancy, the idea is to take the best aspects of centralized and distributed systems and combine them into a hybrid that offers the best of both worlds. This could potentially yield significant benefits in terms of reducing latency, improving performance, and ensuring data integrity. Mastering Git can be seen as a stepping stone towards understanding these potential future trends.

11.3. Understanding Emerging Trends

While Git is designed to handle large codebases, newer technologies, like machine learning, are pushing the boundaries of what version control can do. As the prevalence of artificial intelligence and machine learning in our everyday lives grows, so does the complexity and size of the data being handled, leading to development of Large File Storage (LFS) systems.

Certainly, LFS is not the only emerging trend; there's also Plastic SCM, SVN, Mercurial, and others, each providing unique features and concepts to address specific needs or shortcomings in the version control domain. By immersing yourself in the depth and breadth of these technologies, you enable yourself to grasp trends, which could become pivotal in the future.

11.4. Version Control Systems of the Future

The future of version control lies not only in improving existing systems, but also innovating new ones. With quantum computing on the horizon, the future may demand version control systems that can handle a quantum leap in data complexity and speed. This could lead to the creation of entirely new version control paradigms, heralding unprecedented change in the industry.

While this future might seem distant, preparing for it necessitates beginning now. By mastering Git along with its many layers, understanding how it intersects with other DevOps practices and keeping tabs on issues in the field, you are not just building skills but enabling yourself to future-proof your knowledge.

Each step that you take is inching you closer to becoming an expert in a field that never ceases to evolve. By constantly updating your skills and staying on top of industry trends, you are making yourself invaluable in a rapidly changing technological world.

Mastering Git is indeed a commendable feat, but as you look forward, consider how you can build on this foundation to advance your career. Investigate emerging technologies, keep an eye on industry trends, and always keep learning. Remember, in software development as in life, the only constant is change.